50 Gourmet Toast Dishes

By: Kelly Johnson

Table of Contents

- Avocado Toast with Poached Egg
- Smoked Salmon and Cream Cheese Toast
- Ricotta, Honey, and Fig Toast
- Caprese Toast with Balsamic Glaze
- Truffle Mushroom and Parmesan Toast
- Whipped Goat Cheese and Roasted Grape Toast
- Prosciutto, Arugula, and Burrata Toast
- Smashed Peas and Mint Toast
- Blue Cheese, Pear, and Walnut Toast
- Pesto and Roasted Tomato Toast
- Brie and Caramelized Apple Toast
- Spicy Tuna and Sesame Toast
- Scrambled Egg and Caviar Toast
- Roasted Garlic and Hummus Toast
- Mediterranean Feta and Olive Toast
- Shrimp and Avocado Toast
- Chorizo and Manchego Toast
- Smoked Trout and Dill Toast
- Dark Chocolate and Raspberry Toast
- Lemon Ricotta and Pistachio Toast
- Crab and Avocado Toast
- Balsamic Strawberry and Mascarpone Toast
- Korean Bulgogi and Kimchi Toast
- Sweet Potato and Tahini Toast
- Roasted Red Pepper and Labneh Toast
- Greek Yogurt and Granola Toast
- Cinnamon Sugar and Almond Butter Toast
- Roasted Beet and Herbed Ricotta Toast
- Curried Chicken Salad Toast
- Brie, Prosciutto, and Fig Jam Toast
- Cheddar, Apple, and Maple Bacon Toast
- Spicy Sriracha and Egg Toast
- Mango and Coconut Cream Toast
- Pumpkin Butter and Pecan Toast
- Crab Cake and Remoulade Toast

- Caramelized Onion and Gruyère Toast
- Burrata and Roasted Cherry Toast
- Tandoori Chicken and Cucumber Raita Toast
- Pulled Pork and Pickled Slaw Toast
- Strawberry Basil and Cream Cheese Toast
- Miso Butter and Scallion Toast
- Roasted Cauliflower and Tahini Toast
- Lobster and Herb Butter Toast
- Saffron Honey and Ricotta Toast
- Peking Duck and Hoisin Sauce Toast
- BBQ Jackfruit and Avocado Toast
- Mango Chutney and Brie Toast
- Caviar and Crème Fraîche Toast
- Kimchi and Peanut Butter Toast
- Chocolate Hazelnut and Banana Toast

Avocado Toast with Poached Egg

Ingredients:

- 2 slices sourdough bread, toasted
- 1 ripe avocado, mashed
- 2 eggs
- 1 tablespoon white vinegar
- Salt and pepper to taste
- Red pepper flakes (optional)

Instructions:

1. Bring a pot of water to a gentle simmer and add white vinegar.
2. Crack an egg into a small bowl, then carefully slide it into the simmering water. Repeat with the second egg.
3. Poach for 3-4 minutes, then remove with a slotted spoon.
4. Spread mashed avocado on toast and season with salt and pepper.
5. Top each toast with a poached egg and sprinkle with red pepper flakes.

Smoked Salmon and Cream Cheese Toast

Ingredients:

- 2 slices rye bread, toasted
- 4 tablespoons cream cheese
- 4 ounces smoked salmon
- 1 tablespoon capers
- 1 teaspoon fresh dill, chopped
- Lemon wedges for garnish

Instructions:

1. Spread cream cheese evenly on toasted bread.
2. Layer smoked salmon on top.
3. Sprinkle with capers and fresh dill.
4. Serve with a squeeze of lemon.

Ricotta, Honey, and Fig Toast

Ingredients:

- 2 slices whole grain bread, toasted
- ½ cup ricotta cheese
- 4 fresh figs, sliced
- 2 tablespoons honey
- 1 teaspoon crushed walnuts (optional)

Instructions:

1. Spread ricotta on toasted bread.
2. Arrange fig slices on top.
3. Drizzle with honey and sprinkle with walnuts.

Caprese Toast with Balsamic Glaze

Ingredients:

- 2 slices ciabatta bread, toasted
- 1 fresh mozzarella ball, sliced
- 1 large tomato, sliced
- 4 fresh basil leaves
- 2 tablespoons balsamic glaze
- 1 tablespoon olive oil
- Salt and pepper to taste

Instructions:

1. Layer mozzarella and tomato slices on toast.
2. Add fresh basil leaves.
3. Drizzle with balsamic glaze and olive oil.
4. Season with salt and pepper.

Truffle Mushroom and Parmesan Toast

Ingredients:

- 2 slices baguette, toasted
- 1 cup mushrooms, sliced
- 1 tablespoon butter
- 1 teaspoon truffle oil
- 2 tablespoons grated Parmesan cheese
- Salt and pepper to taste

Instructions:

1. Sauté mushrooms in butter over medium heat until golden brown.
2. Add truffle oil, salt, and pepper.
3. Spoon mushrooms onto toasted bread.
4. Sprinkle with Parmesan cheese before serving.

Whipped Goat Cheese and Roasted Grape Toast

Ingredients:

- 2 slices multigrain bread, toasted
- ½ cup goat cheese, whipped
- 1 cup red grapes
- 1 tablespoon olive oil
- 1 teaspoon honey
- ½ teaspoon fresh thyme

Instructions:

1. Preheat oven to 375°F (190°C).
2. Toss grapes with olive oil and roast for 15 minutes.
3. Spread whipped goat cheese on toast.
4. Top with roasted grapes and drizzle with honey.
5. Garnish with fresh thyme.

Prosciutto, Arugula, and Burrata Toast

Ingredients:

- 2 slices country bread, toasted
- ½ cup burrata cheese, torn
- 4 slices prosciutto
- ½ cup fresh arugula
- 1 tablespoon olive oil
- Black pepper to taste

Instructions:

1. Spread burrata on toasted bread.
2. Layer with prosciutto and arugula.
3. Drizzle with olive oil and sprinkle with black pepper.

Smashed Peas and Mint Toast

Ingredients:

- 2 slices rye bread, toasted
- ½ cup fresh or frozen peas, mashed
- 1 tablespoon lemon juice
- 2 tablespoons crumbled feta cheese
- 2 teaspoons fresh mint, chopped
- Salt and pepper to taste

Instructions:

1. Mix mashed peas with lemon juice, salt, and pepper.
2. Spread onto toasted bread.
3. Sprinkle with crumbled feta and fresh mint.

Blue Cheese, Pear, and Walnut Toast

Ingredients:

- 2 slices walnut bread, toasted
- 2 tablespoons blue cheese, crumbled
- ½ pear, thinly sliced
- 2 tablespoons toasted walnuts
- 1 teaspoon honey

Instructions:

1. Spread blue cheese on toasted bread.
2. Arrange pear slices on top.
3. Sprinkle with walnuts and drizzle with honey.

Pesto and Roasted Tomato Toast

Ingredients:

- 2 slices focaccia, toasted
- 2 tablespoons basil pesto
- ½ cup cherry tomatoes, roasted
- 2 tablespoons fresh basil leaves

Instructions:

1. Spread pesto on toasted focaccia.
2. Top with roasted cherry tomatoes.
3. Garnish with fresh basil leaves.

Brie and Caramelized Apple Toast

Ingredients:

- 2 slices sourdough bread, toasted
- 4 slices Brie cheese
- 1 apple, thinly sliced
- 1 tablespoon butter
- 1 tablespoon brown sugar
- ½ teaspoon cinnamon
- 1 teaspoon honey (optional)

Instructions:

1. Melt butter in a pan over medium heat.
2. Add apple slices, brown sugar, and cinnamon.
3. Sauté for 5 minutes until caramelized.
4. Layer Brie slices on toast, then top with warm apples.
5. Drizzle with honey if desired.

Spicy Tuna and Sesame Toast

Ingredients:

- 2 slices sourdough bread, toasted
- 1 can tuna, drained
- 2 tablespoons mayonnaise
- 1 teaspoon Sriracha (adjust to taste)
- 1 teaspoon soy sauce
- 1 teaspoon sesame seeds
- 1 green onion, chopped

Instructions:

1. Mix tuna, mayonnaise, Sriracha, and soy sauce in a bowl.
2. Spread the mixture on toasted bread.
3. Sprinkle with sesame seeds and chopped green onion.

Scrambled Egg and Caviar Toast

Ingredients:

- 2 slices brioche or sourdough bread, toasted
- 2 eggs
- 1 tablespoon butter
- 1 tablespoon heavy cream
- Salt and pepper to taste
- 1 tablespoon caviar
- Fresh chives for garnish

Instructions:

1. Whisk eggs with heavy cream, salt, and pepper.
2. Cook over low heat with butter, stirring constantly, until soft and creamy.
3. Spread scrambled eggs on toast.
4. Top with caviar and chopped chives.

Roasted Garlic and Hummus Toast

Ingredients:

- 2 slices whole grain bread, toasted
- ½ cup hummus
- 1 head garlic
- 1 tablespoon olive oil
- Salt and pepper to taste
- Fresh parsley for garnish

Instructions:

1. Preheat oven to 400°F (200°C).
2. Cut the top off the garlic head, drizzle with olive oil, and wrap in foil.
3. Roast for 40 minutes until soft.
4. Squeeze roasted garlic cloves into the hummus and mix well.
5. Spread on toast and garnish with parsley.

Mediterranean Feta and Olive Toast

Ingredients:

- 2 slices ciabatta, toasted
- ½ cup crumbled feta cheese
- ¼ cup mixed olives, chopped
- 1 tablespoon olive oil
- 1 teaspoon dried oregano
- Cherry tomatoes, halved

Instructions:

1. Mix feta cheese with olive oil and oregano.
2. Spread on toasted bread.
3. Top with chopped olives and cherry tomatoes.

Shrimp and Avocado Toast

Ingredients:

- 2 slices sourdough bread, toasted
- ½ avocado, mashed
- 6 cooked shrimp, chopped
- 1 teaspoon lime juice
- ½ teaspoon chili flakes
- Salt and pepper to taste
- Fresh cilantro for garnish

Instructions:

1. Mix shrimp with lime juice, chili flakes, salt, and pepper.
2. Spread mashed avocado on toast.
3. Top with shrimp and garnish with cilantro.

Chorizo and Manchego Toast

Ingredients:

- 2 slices baguette, toasted
- 4 slices cured chorizo
- ¼ cup shredded Manchego cheese
- 1 tablespoon honey

Instructions:

1. Layer chorizo on toast.
2. Sprinkle Manchego cheese on top.
3. Drizzle with honey before serving.

Smoked Trout and Dill Toast

Ingredients:

- 2 slices rye bread, toasted
- ½ cup smoked trout, flaked
- 2 tablespoons cream cheese
- 1 teaspoon lemon juice
- 1 teaspoon fresh dill, chopped

Instructions:

1. Mix cream cheese with lemon juice and fresh dill.
2. Spread on toast.
3. Top with flaked smoked trout.

Dark Chocolate and Raspberry Toast

Ingredients:

- 2 slices brioche, toasted
- ¼ cup dark chocolate, melted
- ½ cup fresh raspberries
- 1 teaspoon honey

Instructions:

1. Spread melted dark chocolate on toast.
2. Top with fresh raspberries.
3. Drizzle with honey.

Lemon Ricotta and Pistachio Toast

Ingredients:

- 2 slices whole wheat bread, toasted
- ½ cup ricotta cheese
- 1 teaspoon lemon zest
- 1 tablespoon honey
- 2 tablespoons crushed pistachios

Instructions:

1. Mix ricotta with lemon zest.
2. Spread on toast.
3. Drizzle with honey and sprinkle with pistachios.

Crab and Avocado Toast

Ingredients:

- 2 slices sourdough bread, toasted
- ½ cup lump crab meat
- ½ avocado, mashed
- 1 teaspoon lemon juice
- 1 teaspoon olive oil
- Salt and pepper to taste

Instructions:

1. Mix crab meat with lemon juice, olive oil, salt, and pepper.
2. Spread mashed avocado on toast.
3. Top with crab mixture.

Balsamic Strawberry and Mascarpone Toast

Ingredients:

- 2 slices multigrain bread, toasted
- ½ cup mascarpone cheese
- ½ cup fresh strawberries, sliced
- 1 tablespoon balsamic glaze
- 1 teaspoon honey

Instructions:

1. Spread mascarpone on toast.
2. Arrange sliced strawberries on top.
3. Drizzle with balsamic glaze and honey.

Korean Bulgogi and Kimchi Toast

Ingredients:

- 2 slices sourdough bread, toasted
- ½ cup bulgogi beef, cooked
- ¼ cup kimchi, chopped
- 1 teaspoon sesame seeds
- 1 green onion, chopped
- 1 teaspoon gochujang mayo (optional)

Instructions:

1. Spread gochujang mayo on toast (if using).
2. Layer bulgogi beef and chopped kimchi.
3. Garnish with sesame seeds and chopped green onion.

Sweet Potato and Tahini Toast

Ingredients:

- 2 slices whole wheat bread, toasted
- ½ cup mashed roasted sweet potato
- 1 tablespoon tahini
- 1 teaspoon maple syrup
- ½ teaspoon cinnamon
- Toasted sesame seeds for garnish

Instructions:

1. Mix mashed sweet potato with tahini, maple syrup, and cinnamon.
2. Spread on toast.
3. Sprinkle with toasted sesame seeds.

Roasted Red Pepper and Labneh Toast

Ingredients:

- 2 slices multigrain bread, toasted
- ½ cup labneh
- ½ cup roasted red peppers, chopped
- 1 teaspoon olive oil
- ½ teaspoon smoked paprika
- Fresh parsley for garnish

Instructions:

1. Spread labneh on toast.
2. Top with roasted red peppers.
3. Drizzle with olive oil and sprinkle with smoked paprika.
4. Garnish with fresh parsley.

Greek Yogurt and Granola Toast

Ingredients:

- 2 slices whole grain bread, toasted
- ½ cup Greek yogurt
- ¼ cup granola
- 1 tablespoon honey
- Fresh berries for topping

Instructions:

1. Spread Greek yogurt on toast.
2. Sprinkle with granola.
3. Drizzle with honey and top with fresh berries.

Cinnamon Sugar and Almond Butter Toast

Ingredients:

- 2 slices sourdough bread, toasted
- 2 tablespoons almond butter
- 1 teaspoon cinnamon
- 1 teaspoon coconut sugar
- 1 teaspoon chopped almonds (optional)

Instructions:

1. Spread almond butter on toast.
2. Mix cinnamon and coconut sugar and sprinkle on top.
3. Add chopped almonds for extra crunch.

Roasted Beet and Herbed Ricotta Toast

Ingredients:

- 2 slices rye bread, toasted
- ½ cup ricotta cheese
- ½ teaspoon fresh thyme
- ½ teaspoon lemon zest
- ½ cup roasted beets, sliced
- 1 teaspoon balsamic glaze

Instructions:

1. Mix ricotta with thyme and lemon zest.
2. Spread on toast.
3. Layer with roasted beet slices.
4. Drizzle with balsamic glaze.

Curried Chicken Salad Toast

Ingredients:

- 2 slices whole grain bread, toasted
- ½ cup cooked chicken, shredded
- 1 tablespoon Greek yogurt
- 1 teaspoon curry powder
- 1 teaspoon honey
- 1 tablespoon chopped almonds
- 1 tablespoon chopped raisins

Instructions:

1. Mix chicken, yogurt, curry powder, honey, almonds, and raisins.
2. Spread onto toast.

Brie, Prosciutto, and Fig Jam Toast

Ingredients:

- 2 slices baguette, toasted
- 4 slices Brie cheese
- 2 slices prosciutto
- 2 tablespoons fig jam

Instructions:

1. Spread fig jam on toast.
2. Layer with Brie and prosciutto.

Cheddar, Apple, and Maple Bacon Toast

Ingredients:

- 2 slices country bread, toasted
- 4 slices sharp cheddar cheese
- ½ apple, thinly sliced
- 2 slices maple-glazed bacon, crumbled

Instructions:

1. Layer cheddar and apple slices on toast.
2. Sprinkle with crumbled maple bacon.

Spicy Sriracha and Egg Toast

Ingredients:

- 2 slices sourdough bread, toasted
- 2 fried eggs
- 1 tablespoon Sriracha
- ½ teaspoon sesame seeds
- 1 green onion, chopped

Instructions:

1. Cook eggs to your preference.
2. Place on toast and drizzle with Sriracha.
3. Garnish with sesame seeds and green onion.

Mango and Coconut Cream Toast

Ingredients:

- 2 slices brioche, toasted
- ½ cup coconut cream
- ½ mango, sliced
- 1 teaspoon honey
- 1 tablespoon shredded coconut

Instructions:

1. Spread coconut cream on toast.
2. Layer with mango slices.
3. Drizzle with honey and sprinkle with shredded coconut.

Pumpkin Butter and Pecan Toast

Ingredients:

- 2 slices whole grain bread, toasted
- ¼ cup pumpkin butter
- 2 tablespoons chopped pecans
- 1 teaspoon maple syrup
- ½ teaspoon cinnamon

Instructions:

1. Spread pumpkin butter on toast.
2. Sprinkle with chopped pecans and cinnamon.
3. Drizzle with maple syrup before serving.

Crab Cake and Remoulade Toast

Ingredients:

- 2 slices sourdough bread, toasted
- 2 small crab cakes, cooked
- 2 tablespoons remoulade sauce
- 1 teaspoon fresh parsley, chopped
- Lemon wedges for garnish

Instructions:

1. Place cooked crab cakes on toast.
2. Drizzle with remoulade sauce.
3. Garnish with parsley and serve with lemon wedges.

Caramelized Onion and Gruyère Toast

Ingredients:

- 2 slices baguette, toasted
- 1 cup caramelized onions
- ½ cup shredded Gruyère cheese
- 1 teaspoon fresh thyme

Instructions:

1. Spread caramelized onions on toast.
2. Sprinkle with Gruyère cheese.
3. Broil until cheese is melted and bubbly.
4. Garnish with fresh thyme.

Burrata and Roasted Cherry Tomato Toast

Ingredients:

- 2 slices ciabatta, toasted
- ½ cup burrata cheese
- ½ cup cherry tomatoes, roasted
- 1 tablespoon balsamic glaze
- Fresh basil leaves

Instructions:

1. Spread burrata on toast.
2. Top with roasted cherry tomatoes.
3. Drizzle with balsamic glaze and garnish with basil.

Tandoori Chicken and Cucumber Raita Toast

Ingredients:

- 2 slices naan or sourdough, toasted
- ½ cup cooked tandoori chicken, shredded
- ¼ cup cucumber raita
- Fresh cilantro for garnish

Instructions:

1. Spread cucumber raita on toast.
2. Top with tandoori chicken.
3. Garnish with fresh cilantro.

Pulled Pork and Pickled Slaw Toast

Ingredients:

- 2 slices Texas toast or brioche, toasted
- ½ cup pulled pork, heated
- ¼ cup pickled slaw
- 1 tablespoon barbecue sauce

Instructions:

1. Spread barbecue sauce on toast.
2. Add pulled pork and pickled slaw on top.

Strawberry Basil and Cream Cheese Toast

Ingredients:

- 2 slices whole wheat bread, toasted
- 4 tablespoons cream cheese
- ½ cup fresh strawberries, sliced
- 1 tablespoon honey
- 1 teaspoon fresh basil, chopped

Instructions:

1. Spread cream cheese on toast.
2. Top with sliced strawberries.
3. Drizzle with honey and sprinkle with basil.

Miso Butter and Scallion Toast

Ingredients:

- 2 slices rye bread, toasted
- 2 tablespoons miso butter (1 tbsp miso paste + 1 tbsp butter, mixed)
- 1 scallion, thinly sliced
- ½ teaspoon sesame seeds

Instructions:

1. Spread miso butter on toast.
2. Sprinkle with sliced scallions and sesame seeds.

Roasted Cauliflower and Tahini Toast

Ingredients:

- 2 slices sourdough bread, toasted
- ½ cup roasted cauliflower florets
- 2 tablespoons tahini
- ½ teaspoon smoked paprika
- 1 teaspoon lemon juice

Instructions:

1. Spread tahini on toast.
2. Top with roasted cauliflower.
3. Sprinkle with smoked paprika and drizzle with lemon juice.

Lobster and Herb Butter Toast

Ingredients:

- 2 slices brioche, toasted
- ½ cup cooked lobster meat
- 2 tablespoons herb butter (butter mixed with parsley, garlic, and lemon zest)
- 1 teaspoon chives, chopped

Instructions:

1. Spread herb butter on toast.
2. Top with lobster meat.
3. Garnish with chopped chives.

Saffron Honey and Ricotta Toast

Ingredients:

- 2 slices baguette, toasted
- ½ cup ricotta cheese
- 1 tablespoon saffron-infused honey
- 1 teaspoon crushed pistachios

Instructions:

1. Spread ricotta on toast.
2. Drizzle with saffron-infused honey.
3. Sprinkle with pistachios.

Peking Duck and Hoisin Sauce Toast

Ingredients:

- 2 slices Chinese milk bread or baguette, toasted
- ½ cup shredded Peking duck
- 1 tablespoon hoisin sauce
- 1 tablespoon sliced green onions
- 1 teaspoon sesame seeds

Instructions:

1. Spread hoisin sauce on toast.
2. Top with shredded Peking duck.
3. Garnish with green onions and sesame seeds.

BBQ Jackfruit and Avocado Toast

Ingredients:

- 2 slices sourdough bread, toasted
- ½ cup cooked BBQ jackfruit
- ½ avocado, mashed
- 1 teaspoon lime juice
- ½ teaspoon chili flakes (optional)
- Fresh cilantro for garnish

Instructions:

1. Mash avocado with lime juice and spread on toast.
2. Top with BBQ jackfruit.
3. Sprinkle with chili flakes and garnish with cilantro.

Mango Chutney and Brie Toast

Ingredients:

- 2 slices multigrain bread, toasted
- 4 slices Brie cheese
- 2 tablespoons mango chutney
- 1 teaspoon chopped almonds (optional)

Instructions:

1. Place Brie slices on toast.
2. Spoon mango chutney over the cheese.
3. Sprinkle with chopped almonds if desired.

Caviar and Crème Fraîche Toast

Ingredients:

- 2 slices blini or brioche, toasted
- 2 tablespoons crème fraîche
- 1 tablespoon caviar
- ½ teaspoon lemon zest
- Fresh chives for garnish

Instructions:

1. Spread crème fraîche on toast.
2. Top with caviar.
3. Garnish with lemon zest and chopped chives.

Kimchi and Peanut Butter Toast

Ingredients:

- 2 slices rye bread, toasted
- 2 tablespoons peanut butter
- ¼ cup kimchi, chopped
- 1 teaspoon sesame seeds
- ½ teaspoon honey

Instructions:

1. Spread peanut butter on toast.
2. Top with chopped kimchi.
3. Sprinkle with sesame seeds and drizzle with honey.

Chocolate Hazelnut and Banana Toast

Ingredients:

- 2 slices sourdough bread, toasted
- 2 tablespoons chocolate hazelnut spread
- 1 banana, sliced
- 1 teaspoon crushed hazelnuts
- ½ teaspoon cinnamon (optional)

Instructions:

1. Spread chocolate hazelnut spread on toast.
2. Arrange banana slices on top.
3. Sprinkle with crushed hazelnuts and cinnamon.

www.ingramcontent.com/pod-product-compliance
Lightning Source LLC
LaVergne TN
LVHW081338060526
838201LV00055B/2720